Tips From Widowers

Also by Jan Robinson

Tips From Widows

Tips From Widowers

Jan Robinson

BLOOMSBURY
LONDON · OXFORD · NEW YORK · NEW DELHI · SYDNEY

Bloomsbury Publishing
An imprint of Bloomsbury Publishing Plc

50 Bedford Square
London
WC1B 3DP
UK

1385 Broadway
New York
NY 10018
USA

www.bloomsbury.com

BLOOMSBURY and the Diana logo are trademarks of Bloomsbury Publishing Plc

First published in Great Britain 2016

© Jan Robinson, 2016

Jan Robinson has asserted her right under the Copyright, Designs and
Patents Act, 1988, to be identified as Author of this work.

British Library Cataloguing-in-Publication Data
A catalogue record for this book is available from the British Library.

ISBN: HB: 978-1-4088-7809-5
ePub: 978-1-4088-7810-1

2 4 6 8 10 9 7 5 3 1

Typeset by Newgen Knowledge Works (P) Ltd., Chennai, India
Printed and bound in Great Britain by CPI Group (UK) Ltd, Croydon CR0 4YY

To find out more about our authors and books visit www.bloomsbury.com.
Here you will find extracts, author interviews, details of forthcoming
events and the option to sign up for our newsletters.

This book is dedicated to all
those who have loved and lost

Contents

Foreword   ix

Preface   xi

Part I: **Before she dies**   1
            Money I   3
            Not quite a widower   6

Part II   **When she dies**   9
            Funeral director   11
            Registrar   12
            Funeral   13
            Letter writing   15
            Afterlife   16
            Accountant   17

Part III   **The months after she dies**   19
            Love and loss: the symptoms   21
            Love and loss: dealing with loss   25
            Other people's reactions   28
            Children   30
            Young widowers and children   31
            Grandchildren   33
            Crying and psychological higher
            education   34
            Flashbacks   35
            Anger   36
            Guilt   37
            House and home   38
            Emergencies   42
            Money II   43

	Walking	44
	Going alone	46
	Miscellaneous thoughts and maxims	47
Part IV	**The years after she dies**	**51**
	Remembering	53
	Consolations	55
	Dating and remarriage	56
	Quiche & crampons: 'wolves surrounding the laager'	59
	Remarriage and your children	61
Part V	**When you die**	**63**
	A practical approach to your own death	65
Appendix		**71**
	Gifts	73
	Joint bank accounts	74
	Your accountant	75
Acknowledgements		**77**
Poems		**81**
	On the death of Elizabeth Soane	83
	Ode to Kath	84
	Untitled	85
	Splendour in the Grass	86
	Baucis and Philemon	87
For your notes		**89**

Foreword

When my wife Siân Busby died in 2012, I was overwhelmed by the affection and kindness showered on me by friends and family. But I also felt alone and a bit lost. The point, which anyone widowed will immediately get, is that it is bewildering to have to deal with probably the most traumatic event of your life, and not be able to turn for help and advice to the person on whom you have been leaning for years and decades, your adored dead partner.

There is so much with which to come to terms and sort. In my case – and for many – there are all the responsibilities of suddenly becoming a single parent. There is the tidal wave of grief that hits you and those close to you, and can make you go somewhat bonkers for a while. And there is a mountain of stressful and tedious administration that is precipitated by any death: from registering it to organising the funeral, dealing with banks and credit-card companies, administering the will, and so on.

What I learned is that because on the whole people live much longer than they did even a generation or two back, as a society we've lost the habit of knowing how to help widows and widowers. I was struck when reading the book *The Cruel Mother*, written by my late wife about her own great-grandmother, that a century ago communities rallied around and supported the bereaved in a much more effective and practical way than is true today.

So Jan's little book for widowers should be seen as compensating in part for how we've lost the habit of death. Now, to be clear, I don't agree with all her prescriptions and tips, and you should not necessarily adopt them all. Every bereavement, every widowing is different. As widows and widowers, we all have much in common, but each one of us is unique, too.

That said, we all could do with advice when our wives die, because there is no dress rehearsal for becoming a widower. Think of this book as a wise and practically minded friend when you need one most.

Robert Peston
December 2015

Preface

A couple of years ago I put together a small volume entitled *Tips From Widows*. This was not because I was in any way an expert on widowhood but because, being a widow myself, I had heard so many stories from other widows. These had helped me immeasurably, so I had the idea of collecting them and putting them in book form.

Small though it was, the book generated a huge response, not only from widows, but also from widowers, who wrote to me in large numbers, and before long it became clear to me that a second book, this time for widowers, was inevitable.

I have been surprised and also moved to receive all sorts of communications from widowers of various ages telling me their stories and often letting me into their innermost thoughts. As I have said before, grief is an unmanageable emotion, and it takes a different form with every person, whether man or woman. Nevertheless, a number of constant themes emerge, and there are certainly a few indisputable dos and don'ts collected and concentrated in this book.

Although widows and widowers share many similar experiences in bereavement, leading to many similar feelings, there are differences in the ways men cope with this state. It is a sobering thought that half the married population of the world will experience the same thing, and yet so few talk about it. Indeed, it is fair to say, as a broad generalisation, that whereas women readily discuss their emotions, men are far less inclined to do so.

While this book is primarily written for widowers who have lost their wives or partners of the opposite sex, much of the advice in it is pertinent to men who have lost same-sex partners. For purely stylistic reasons, and in order to avoid the repetitive overuse of the rather cumbersome expression 'wife or partner', I will often refer simply to the 'wife' or to the 'spouse' or to the 'partner', in most cases using these words interchangeably. It is, as I say, a matter of stylistic convention and nothing more.

A widower who is a retired doctor wrote to me recently and made the point that many older men are, as he put it, 'classically feeble at fending for themselves'; he was referring to simple everyday tasks such as cooking, shopping, washing clothes, or even keeping themselves tidy. This same doctor expressed the view, widely held, that in order to survive, men have for centuries organised society to their advantage, convincing themselves that they are the stronger sex, when all the time they know in their hearts that they are the weaker. 'There's nothing like fooling yourself,' he concluded.

I have heard, again from a widower, that in his opinion – and of course this is the broadest of broad generalisations – women score above men in almost every area apart from physical strength, and that this is also true of how they deal with bereavement. Most men, continued this same widower, dread the thought of being widowed, which is why many middle-aged and elderly widowers remarry in haste, often to regret at leisure. Marriage without love is a cold union, and this widower knew a number of couples who had married for companionship and looked as miserable as sin. Another widower had found the whole experience of bereavement so unbearable that the only advice he had to offer spouses of either sex was: 'Die first.'

Whilst the purpose of this book is mainly to offer practical advice to men who are going through a devastating period, I do hope that some of its contents might provoke a smile or two. Furthermore, although the tips offered here are primarily intended for middle-aged or elderly widowers, there is also a section of tips and advice for two other categories. Firstly, young widowers. And secondly, older men, generally married for many years, whose wives have developed severe dementia or some similar degenerative condition, so that the man is a widower to all intents and purposes, although not free to act as one.

At the end of this book there are a few spare pages for you to add any further tips and useful sayings.

Finally, in order to make the point that widowerhood does not have to be associated only with loss and gloom, but that it can also offer opportunities, even later in life, let us look at the word itself and spell out a few more positive associations. Despite his loss – and perhaps even thanks to it – the widower might ideally be described as follows:

W	wise
I	insightful
D	decent
O	open
W	willing
E	entertaining
R	reliable

In other words, whilst I fully recognise that the experience of widowerhood contains much that is difficult to the point of being unbearable, it is not, I hope, trivial or condescending to suggest that the future can hold something of value.

Part I

Before she dies

Money I

If it is clear that your wife will not live for much longer, it is important to talk to her about the financial implications of her passing away. Some wives will be quite happy to do this. Others might need to be encouraged.

> **Tip 1** Encourage each other to talk about these matters well before either person has become too ill to do so.

It is essential to have a joint account with your wife. (For more details, see the Appendix, page 74.)

The moment your wife dies, any bank account that's in her name only will immediately and automatically be frozen, even if you are the sole beneficiary of her will. So if, say, your wife was responsible for all matters relating to household bills, and if she managed these using an account in her name only, you will be unable to access any money at all from this account.

This is what happens by law. Specifically, any account in your wife's sole name will remain frozen from the moment she dies until probate is complete; and this process often lasts up to six months, and can last even longer. Note, too, that all Direct Debit payments that have been set up for this account will also stop immediately; so if Direct Debits for your household bills go through an account solely in the name of your wife, your entire life will quite literally come to a halt.

Tip 2 It is *absolutely essential* to do one of the following two things:

Set up a joint account with your wife, and make sure that all Direct Debit payments for your family and household go through this account (and not through an account in your wife's name only).

Set aside a sum that you know will be sufficient to carry you through the worst-case probate scenario.

Bear in mind, too, that many people find that the paperwork resulting from the death of a wife or partner is overwhelming. If, added to this, your wife was the one who ran the house and paid all the bills, the paperwork will be even worse. In this case, it might be advisable to find a reliable and competent friend who lives close by and who can come round and help you with the mountains of administration in the first three months.

It is also vital to think about pensions. To put it bluntly, if you and your partner have simply been co-habiting for a long time and are not married, after her death you will not be regarded as her legal widower, and will be unable to receive any widower's state pension. However, your partner will very probably be able to nominate you as the beneficiary of her workplace pension after her death.

Tip 3 Only if it is what you both wish, get married or become civil partners! Do so at once; or at least make the appropriate pension nomination if that is what you both want.

Not quite a widower

A friend of mine introduced me to a married man who came to my home to talk about his wife, who has dementia and only occasionally recognises him. When her life started to close in around her and her behaviour became more and more unreliable, he found himself doing absolutely everything for her – including bathing her. She is now safely in a home, where she is well looked after in a secure and well-ordered environment.

The not-quite widower said that in the years before this, he tried, unsuccessfully, to give her other experiences outside their home, which he hoped would stimulate her. However, this made her even more fearful and also occasionally caused her to become violent and antisocial, which was upsetting for all involved. Finally, it was the joint decision taken by this man and his adult children to find a suitable home for her.

He still feels that he could have done more for her, but at least he now realises that if he kept her at home for longer than was advisable, it was partly out of love, and partly, too, because he was in denial of her true state, which he now recognises. In the end, it was his children who made him face facts.

Counsellors helped him and his children to try to understand the cruel world of dementia. He has been married for many years and is grateful for the life he and his wife had together before the onset of this disease. He would like to 'move on', as he puts it, but feels guilty about thinking this way. When he meets single women, he has to explain to them that a serious relationship is out of the question, if only because he is still grieving for the life that he previously enjoyed with his wife. As a result, he is very lonely and is stuck in a no man's land. Unfortunately, there is no way out of his predicament. Perhaps other men who are not quite widowers may feel able to choose other options.

Tip If your wife has dementia, it is in her own best interests that she should eventually be looked after in a home.

Part II

When she dies

Funeral director

All the information and help you need will be provided by the funeral director just after the death of your wife, and he or she will guide you through everything you need to know. If you know your wife is dying, do choose a funeral director you feel is sympathetic to the requirements of both spouses. In the event of her sudden death, this will, of course, not be possible.

It is so easy, with the emotional turmoil, to forget to tell the funeral director to let you know, after the cremation, when the casket will be available to be collected.

Tip 1   If your wife has been cremated, consider keeping her ashes for some later moment; for example, to be scattered in the same place with your ashes when your own time comes.

Tip 2   Whatever you decide to do with your wife's ashes, keeping the urn on show in your home sometimes creates problems with family and visitors, so discretion is advisable.

Registrar

Registering the death of your wife can be a very painful experience, so take along a friend or relative, since with your emotions awry, you will probably not be able to concentrate. You will be given printed material, including information about immediate cancellations that are required for your new status. You don't have to remember much of what the registrar says, because he or she will talk you through it. It is a legal process that has to be done, and you should be aware that it will be upsetting.

Tip 1 Take a friend.

The registrar will, as a matter of course, give you a death certificate, and will also ask you whether you would like further copies, which will be official documents, not standard photocopies. Do be sure to take this opportunity to ask for copies of this vital document. A whole range of professionals will require it, and photocopies won't do. The document, I repeat, must be generated by the registrar.

Tip 2 Be sure to get *at least half-a-dozen* copies of your wife's death certificate from the registrar.

Funeral

Some religions traditionally lay down that the funeral should take place immediately after death. Others, on the other hand, allow more time. In this case, whether you have a church service or a service at a crematorium, or both, you can therefore think about the way you wish things to be done.

Sometimes, after the death of your wife, a post-mortem may be required by law. This can delay the burial or cremation, and you will have to wait until the body is released to the funeral director. This can be most upsetting, but there is no getting round it.

Tip 1 Do involve your children in all the arrangements and decisions with regard to the funeral arrangements for their mother; also, take your time.

Tip 2 Do encourage grandchildren to go to the funeral or cremation. In the case of very young children, it is for the parents to decide whether they should attend.

Tip 3 In the very early days following your wife's death, the phone will ring constantly. The emotional strain of answering every call will often be too great. It is therefore a good idea to use voicemail or switch on your answerphone whenever you feel like it; or, alternatively, to get a friend or adult child to answer on your behalf.

Letter writing

It is a broad generalisation, but many men find it easier to address their loss by writing, rather than by talking. Indeed, one newly widowed man found it impossible to tell people that his wife had died, and asked his friends to spread the news. In any case, many men will probably find that they do want to reply to all or most of the letters of condolence that they receive.

You may or may not receive any number of letters, cards, or even emails of condolence. One bereaved spouse I know received several hundred letters, and was also surprised to receive a number of emails, which at the time seemed rather informal, although they were also comforting, especially since the emails arrived straight away, whereas the letters came in more slowly.

As for the way to reply to these messages, it is really up to you. You might wish to reply to emails with emails, to letters with letters. The choice is yours. You will, however, almost certainly find it impossible to write long letters to everyone who contacts you, and some widowers find it convenient to send out standard cards. There also has to be a cut-off point for replying, and several people have suggested to me that this should be three months after the death of your wife.

Tip In the end, the choice as to whether to reply, and when, is entirely yours.

Afterlife

There are many different views – some religious, others not – about what will happen to your wife after she dies. Does she exist in some form? Can she hear me? Or does she perhaps not exist in any form at all? Your perception or your belief is your own truth. You may change your views, but do not let anyone else tell you what to believe. Some bereaved people have told me that they walk round their home talking to their dead spouse in the belief that the departed can hear them.

One widower was convinced that his dead partner had not really left him. 'I had the feeling that sometimes he was there with me, supporting and encouraging me,' he wrote. 'He had been an artist his whole life, and after his death I began making stone sculptures myself.'

Accountant

If you have an accountant, do not change accountancy firms during the first year of widowerhood. If you do, it might appear to the Inland Revenue as an indication that you are perhaps trying to avoid paying the full tax you owe.

For example (and this story applies to widows and widowers), a recently widowed woman aged sixty-three was asked by the Inland Revenue to produce a record of all monies received and paid by her and her husband over the previous seven years. The Inland Revenue had no reason to suspect any wrongdoing at all; nevertheless it is fully within its rights to review all accounts, without providing any reason, going back over seven years. Therefore even though neither the widow nor her recently deceased husband had done anything untoward, and even though their joint accounts were in perfect order, she had to pay her accountant £7,000 to do the job, which involved weeks of painstaking work.

Tip For seven years after you are widowed, take out professional free protection (your accountant can deal with the practicalities) to cover the risk of this happening to you. Approximate annual cost: £80 . . . which is money well spent, considering the possible downside.

If you doubt the wisdom of this tip, bear in mind two things. Firstly, it comes from an experienced accountant who has seen it happen before. Secondly, and more generally, you should be aware that since the country's finances are in a state of some disorder (to say the least!), the taxman is more hungry for your money than ever before.

Part III

The months after she dies

Love and loss: the symptoms

Those who have been blessed by a long marriage or relationship of mutual love know and can remember the indescribable feelings of excessive joy, happiness, and also the realisation that you could hardly live without this person. When you were in this state you radiated love, often to the frustration of others. You were liable to be forgetful, absent-minded, irrational, and even antisocial. Such is the intensity of this experience, both for mind and body, that you usually have time only for yourselves.

Plato describes love as a 'serious mental disease'.

Over a long period of marriage these feelings soften (you can't live on love and a lettuce leaf), and others emerge, such as fondness, contentment, deep friendship, trust and mutual respect.

When you lose your spouse (particularly when the loss is sudden) it is such a shock that at first you cannot cope with this dramatic change, and perhaps sometimes feel you are going round the bend. A widower wrote to me saying that his grief was all-consuming, so much so that he felt it would destroy him. Fighting it was, he said, a 24/7 operation, which was especially demanding at night.

In circumstances of extreme grief your body reacts, physiologically speaking, in a number of ways. Firstly, and to defend itself, the autonomic nervous system (over which we have almost no conscious control) is stimulated to flood the body with adrenalin. This is responsible for many unwanted symptoms such as:

- breathlessness
- chest tightness
- stomach pains
- numbness
- headaches
- dizziness
- loss of appetite or, on the other hand, excessive eating
- weight loss or gain
- palpitations
- loss of libido
- restlessness
- sleep disturbance
- fatigue and involuntary sighing.

Secondly, and to help the body cope, the nervous system stimulates the release of huge amounts of the hormone ACTH (adrenocorticotropic hormone) from the pituitary gland, which in turn encourages the adrenal gland to produce cortisone in large quantities. Unfortunately, cortisone has a detrimental effect on the immune system, so that particularly in prolonged periods of bereavement, individuals become more prone to infections and even to cancer, which is why there is a higher incidence of physical illness in bereaved people.

Prolonged high levels of cortisone also affect the thalamus in the brain, which is the centre for sensory perception. This is what leads to many of the behavioural changes that bereaved people can experience, such as:

- disorganisation
- withdrawal from social situations and work
- absent-mindedness
- forgetfulness
- lack of concentration
- auditory and visual hallucinations (i.e. 'flashbacks')
- vivid dreams
- preoccupation with thoughts of the deceased
- and again, feeling one is losing one's sanity.

What can we do to help these ghastly and sometimes overwhelming physical and mental symptoms? The vital thing is to realise that for most people these excessive feelings are temporary and in most cases will eventually disperse. However, in a few cases, some, including flashbacks, anger, guilt, sadness and even suicidal feelings, can be very prolonged.

If this happens, it is advisable to seek medical and/or psychological assistance by going to see your GP, or contacting a grief counsellor, Cruse Bereavement Care, the Samaritans, Age UK or Silverline.

This level of sadness, universally experienced, is not the same as depression. Freud neatly put it into a single sentence. 'In grief,' he wrote, 'the world looks poor and empty. In depression, the person feels poor and empty.' There is, furthermore, a classic and widely recognised pattern of grief that is experienced by all people who have been bereaved. First, shock; then denial; then anger; and finally, acceptance. This can often take the form of one step forward and two steps back, rather like a game of snakes and ladders. Eventually, however, you can hope to reach the haven of acceptance.

> **Tip** Waking up alone at 4 a.m.: listen to the World Service on Radio 4 or to one of the many all-night talk radio stations.

With regard to consulting a professional figure, one widower told me that this wasn't his 'scene'. He couldn't think of anything worse than discussing his grief with someone who didn't know his wife. The same, he felt, went for GPs, who in his view had many more important matters to deal with.

Whether or not you consult a professional figure is, of course, your choice. However, one advantage of paying a professional to listen to you is that you spare your friends and family this burden; and whilst to begin with your friends will be supportive, it is unwise to put them to the test for too long.

Love and loss: dealing with loss

Much of what follows (and indeed, much of what I have written above) comes from a retired doctor, himself a widower, to whom I owe a debt of thanks for professional opinions and tips that he gave me and that I pass on here.

The way to deal with the excessive amounts of adrenalin and cortisone circulating in the body is to consume them by doing things that stimulate the all-uplifting endorphins in the brain. For example, move your body by going for a walk, either by yourself, with a companion, or with a dog. It is remarkable how beneficial this is. However, walks take time. Alternatively, short, *fairly* high-intensity exercise can have the same effect and has the added benefit, in males, of stimulating the production of testosterone. After the age of forty, all males lose testosterone at the rate of approximately 1 per cent per year. In bereaved males, where the excess of cortisone further reduces the production of testosterone, the levels of this latter hormone drop far more, which accounts (in part) for the reduced libido. Since testosterone is important for guarding against CVS (cardiovascular system) disease, muscle wasting, osteoporosis, depression, dementia, and even death, it is vital to maintain it at a good level.

Other beneficial activities include going to the gym, playing a game such as tennis or badminton, all of which will involve meeting new people with new faces that carry no baggage where bereavement is concerned. Singing and music are also very efficient at lowering cortisone levels. Indeed, members of the Bach Choir in London had their cortisone levels measured before and after a concert. After it, the levels were found to have halved. You do not necessarily have to join a choir. Singing out loud to yourself is just as effective.

There are also many other ways of stimulating production of those all-important endorphins. In normal life, we do this every day by reading a favourite book, for example, or watching telly or listening to the radio; by gardening or pursuing any hobby; or by seeing your children and maybe even your grandchildren.

In this respect, one of the very few undoubted benefits (yes, I mean benefits) of bereavement is that you become single again, which means that you can please yourself. With marriage comes compromise. One widower who contacted me found it most beneficial, as a method of coping with bereavement, to take up some of the interests that he had had as a single man but that a busy job and a full family life had prevented him from pursuing. The things that uniquely interest you are never boring, and now, especially if you have retired from work, you have all the time in the world to do as you please.

You might also think of offering your time to a charity on a voluntary basis. One widower who did this told me that he was snapped up immediately.

All the above are positive activities that require effort, and obviously there are periods when a grieving individual will lack the necessary motivation. At times like this, it is all too tempting to uncork a bottle of wine, open a packet of cigarettes, or even use drugs, whether hard or soft. The easy option is, however, a mistake, and all it does is to numb the brain and to prevent it from slowly readjusting. To indulge in these things often results in withdrawal from society, which in turn leads to increasing loneliness. I do not, of course, wish to deny the considerable pleasure that is provided by a few glasses of wine. What I am talking about here is indulgence to excess. Alcohol is, after all, a depressant, and as such does not offer the solution to the widower's predicament.

> **Tip** Although often difficult, the readjustment to your new status as single man can help you become a new person, perhaps wiser and more *simpatico*. Be prepared to reinvent yourself, to the benefit of yourself and everyone else.

Finally, it should be said that keeping busy is not necessarily the right solution for everyone. 'I didn't feel the need to keep constantly busy,' wrote one widower. 'Constructive moping can be a healer. I felt that death wasn't the end of love, and that the bittersweet going-over of beloved features, events and shared history wasn't maudlin, but that it was, on the other hand, a way of imprinting my wife on my very being. It was a positive comfort immediately after her death, and also *in perpetuam*.'

Other people's reactions

There have probably been times in all of our lives when we have not been able to fully comprehend or empathise with a recently widowed man or woman. Some people cannot find the right words and seem unable to face you. Others may not mention your departed spouse's name, or might not speak to you at all; and others might even cross the road in order to avoid bumping into you. All this is very painful, but the truth is that we never really know what's going on in other people's minds.

For this reason, it's best not to get offended by the comments you'll hear. For example:

'Now that you're back on the market again . . .'
'I know just how you feel. My dog died yesterday.'
'Will you be marrying again?'
'I'm so sorry to hear about [your departed spouse], and I just wanted to tell you: it gets worse.'

Almost invariably, these comments and many others like them – often quite astoundingly inappropriate – are not the result of conscious thought at all. People will often say the first words that come into their minds, however foolish or even offensive.

Tip Do not be offended. They don't mean it.

Lastly, a gay widower whose partner died of cancer wrote to say that many of his friends assumed that his partner had in fact died of AIDS, and were convinced that the poor widower was lying. There wasn't much that he could do to persuade them otherwise.

Children

It is easy to become too self-absorbed in your own grief and if you have adult children they, too, will be feeling the huge loss of their mother and will also be very concerned about you. Although you will be able to share some of your grief with them, it is sometimes difficult – a strange and upsetting time for all involved, with each person's reactions being quite different. For example, one adult son coped with the loss of a father by writing a book about him, including old family photographs. For other children, it can be a consolation to realise that the dead parent will always be with them and in them – after all, half a child's genes come from each parent.

A widower who wrote to me said that mothers and fathers sometimes have quite different ways of talking to their children on the phone. He said that after his wife died, he had to learn the art of 'chatting' to his daughters, something that he had never done before. However, he warned that the surviving husband should not feel that he has to – or even can – provide the day-to-day support and wisdom that had previously come from his wife.

Young widowers and children

I was contacted by a widower in his late thirties who gave me a whole series of tips about dealing with being the sole parent of a young child. They appear here in no particular order.

As he was running his own business, he had to reorganise his working day so as to be able to take his daughter to school and pick her up. He achieved this by learning to delegate, and realised that as a result, not only was he working shorter hours, but he was also working more efficiently than before. He commented that there is more to life than spending long hours in the office.

As a new adventure after his wife's death, he started dinghy-sailing with his daughter in the holidays, and also went camping with her – first in a tent in the garden, then in the country, and then in France.

The hospice that had looked after his wife also helped him and his daughter a great deal. Among other things, they gave him a children's book for him to read to her. This was about an old badger who was dying, about how that was a natural thing to happen, and about how he went to a happy place after he died. This helped him to form an even stronger bond with his daughter, and also helped him to talk with her about the good times they had all had together as a family.

Through Cruse, an organisation for widows, widowers and their children, he and his daughter went on regular outings with other children who had lost a parent, and even spent Christmas holidays with them, which was especially useful, this being a difficult time of the year for single parents. He would never have got involved if it hadn't been for the needs of his daughter, but he wanted her to know that there were many other children in the same situation. 'I found it helped me a lot, too,' he wrote. 'It gave me more confidence in learning how to "chat up the women" again.'

Grandchildren

They, too, need to be comforted and to be able to talk freely about their loss. Allow them to comfort you as well. Encourage them, even if it brings tears to all of you. Their perception of their grandmother will be quite different from their parents' perception of her, and will be a bonus for all the family.

Tip Talk.

A friend said that one of the compensations for the loss of her husband (and this applies just as much to widowers as it does to widows) was to see him replicated in many small ways in her grandchildren. This was a great solace. And a seventy-eight-year-old widower wrote to me to say that he derives much pleasure from helping to look after his twin granddaughters. He also comments that, whether he likes it or not, fetching them involves hanging around primary-school gates, which is a sociable spot and people are happy to have a chat as they wait for the children.

Crying and psychological higher education

Tears are a unique liquid that your body produces. They bathe the soul. You will cry – on and off – for the rest of your life, and the tears will often be triggered by the smallest thing, generally a happy or beautiful memory that might come to you at any time.

A widower said that he wasn't ashamed, or even too concerned, by the fact that he would suddenly burst into tears and 'cry like a baby', as he put it. People seemed to understand.

However, just occasionally both widowers and widows find that the tears will not come. One widow found herself unable to cry. The sudden shock of losing her husband was so intense that she is now seeking the help of a professional therapist.

Tip Don't be surprised to find yourself crying, even after many years.

Flashbacks

It is normal – certainly for a number of months after your wife's death – to have flashbacks to images of her lying dead. These can be very vivid and real, and are always deeply upsetting. If these flashbacks continue for any length of time, you should seek help.

Anger

Anger is often the product of unexpressed hurt, and can have unexpected consequences. For example, one man was so angry at the loss of his wife that his previously strong Catholic faith was severely tested. Another vented his anger at the medical profession in general by writing a strongly worded missive to the hospital that had looked after his wife during her final illness.

Tip If, following the death of your spouse, you are tempted to send angry letters to various parties, it does no harm to write them, but it is in almost all cases better not to send them.

Guilt

You might feel guilty that some old issues with your other half had never been fully discussed, and that now it is too late. Most wives or partners would wish you to make the most of the years that are left to you.

Tip Forgive yourself.

House and home

It would be a mistake to assume that all cooking and household chores are done almost exclusively by women. We all know that some men assume this responsibility during their married lives, and especially after retirement. However, we also all know that some men are worse than clueless in this area, and this section of the book is aimed mainly at them.

One widower tells me that immediately after he was widowed he realised that he would have to familiarise himself with the whereabouts of all the domestic items in the house. He started in the kitchen area and worked his way through all the drawers and cupboards. Especially in the kitchen, he was amazed to find so many useless gadgets that had been accumulated over the years, so he had a good clear-out, keeping only what he thought was necessary, and placing them where he could find them.

> **Tip 1** Clear out your kitchen and keep all items to a minimum. (But, as one widower strongly advised, do keep the slow cooker!)

Many widowers I have spoken to found that the most difficult aspect of the clearing-out process in the months following their wife's death was dealing with her clothes. Whether to keep them, give them to a daughter to go through, or to give them away to a charity, is a difficult decision. All agree, however, that this process should not be done in a hurry, as it will inevitably lead to regrets later.

One young widower was asked by his mother-in-law if he knew the whereabouts of some rather valuable family jewellery, the very existence of which he had been ignorant of. It turned out that his late wife had stashed numerous items in the pockets of her clothing, with brooches pinned to jacket lapels; and that other bits of her jewellery were hidden in various places around the house, including inside pots of dried flowers. Thank goodness he hadn't given the clothes away in a hurry. Similarly, don't throw away mementos, and do keep all photos. If to begin with you find it too painful to look at them, hide them away until later.

Now we come to cooking. As we know, some men love it and are entirely at ease in the kitchen. Others, however, hardly know how to boil an egg, and unless they are rich enough to employ a full-time cook, they will simply have to learn a few basics. The good news here is that you can do it. As the daughter of one widower said to him with a sigh: 'Dad, if you can read, you can cook.' However, for those who do not wish to open even the most simple cookbook, there are always TV cooking programmes, or indeed local cooking courses, which have the added benefit that you get out and meet people. At this stage one should emphasise the importance of eating well, and this does involve some knowledge of how to operate in the kitchen.

One widower wrote to say that he had turned down his daughter's offer of providing frozen meals for him after his wife died, and that he decided to learn to cook for himself and for friends and family. He felt that planning the meal, doing the shopping, laying the table and even clearing up afterwards helped to give a structure to his life, and he also felt that if he let standards slip, it would be the beginning of the end. Indeed, he even continued his wife's habit of making a flower arrangement for the hall table once a week. For others, however, frozen meals are a blessing, as is the microwave. And for those who truly need them, there are always 'meals on wheels' companies.

Elsewhere in the house, you will have to deal with your own laundry. 'You will no doubt learn the hard way,' commented one young widower. 'I thought you just put everything in the washing machine and pressed the button. Wrong! I ended up with my favourite woollen jumpers too small even for my daughter, my cotton shirts much too creased for ironing, and I have now ended up with pink sheets and pink underpants!'

All of the above is nicely summed up in a series of tips given to me by a widower in his nineties:

- Essential: discipline and a regular routine.
- Allocate yourself at least one small task a day to do.
- Try to have one good substantial meal a day.
- Body hygiene: teeth (beware bad breath, flossing will help), shave, change clothes, cut and clean nails, dress decently.

- Keep a diary, even if it only records the weather.
- Read a paper, read books, do the crossword.
- Keep a pride in yourself, do the housework.
- If you have a garden, keep it tidy; feed the birds?
- If possible, get and use a computer.

On a different note, and this applies equally to widows and widowers, if you shared a double bed with your wife, it might be an idea to sleep for one week on your side of the bed, and for one week on hers. I have heard of a widow who found this comforting. It also saves on the laundry!

Some men and women also keep an item that still has the unique smell of their loved one, e.g. a dressing gown or other piece of clothing. You might want to spray some of her scent on your pillow.

Lastly, I have heard the tip that follows again and again, and cannot emphasise its importance enough.

Tip 2 Unless it is an absolute necessity from the financial point of view, do *not* sell your home in the first year of your widowerhood. It is bad enough to lose a spouse, but to add to this the emotional upheaval of a house move is highly inadvisable. I have heard numerous stories of people who made this mistake and then bitterly regretted it.

Emergencies

When you become a widower you will find yourself completely alone, perhaps for the first time, and you will sometimes feel very vulnerable. If any emergency should arise, especially in the first few months, do not hesitate to ask for help, even if that means appealing to other people's better natures.

> **Tip** Don't be afraid to ask for help, and to ask again. It is an opportunity for people to help you, and you would help them too, in very different circumstances.

An elderly widower recently had to go to hospital in the middle of the night, and was quite unprepared for this emergency. He tells me that he now has the following items set aside in a little bag in case anything similar happens again:

- Full list of medication you normally take, along with name and address of your doctor; these are the first things that any ambulance crew wants to know.
- All items that you will need for a short stay in hospital. In other words: pyjamas, dressing gown and slippers; spare underclothes, wash-bag, towel; pen and small amount of money; reading material; duplicate house keys and a spare phone charger.

You should, ideally, always keep about you a list of the medication you take and the name and address of your doctor.

Money II

If, immediately after your wife has died, you are contacted by someone claiming that she owed them money, you must refer this person (no matter how respectable they sound) to your solicitor. The bereaved are prime targets for people claiming money dishonestly, and it is surprising how many of them fall for this familiar scam.

Tip If anyone calls saying your wife owed money and asking for payment, refer that person to your solicitor. No exceptions.

Walking

Walking is famously therapeutic.

One bereaved person aged fifty walked the entire length of Offa's Dyke with a friend, completing the journey in a series of three-day sessions. The exercise, the change of scene, the beauty of the countryside, the physical challenge . . . all these things were immensely beneficial and helped the bereaved person to look outwards towards the world, rather than inwards.

Tip 1 Go for long walks. A good hour's walk a day gets you out, and you always feel better for it.

Tip 2 Even if you don't feel like a walk, it is important to get out every day. So meet up with friends; go out for coffee or meals; anything! It all helps you not to continually focus on your loss. It doesn't stop the grieving process, but it will temporarily distract you, and it is distraction that you need.

Tip 3 The most important muscle in your whole body is your smile.

Tip 4 As mentioned previously, some bereaved people find that having a pet – an animal to hold or stroke – helps enormously. Taking a dog for a walk also enables you to meet other dog owners.

Going alone

There are, by common consent, a number of aspects of bereavement which are quite different for men than they are for women. One of these is the question of your social life after the death of your other half. As a very general rule, widows all too often find that their social life comes to an abrupt halt and that the invitations just stop. However, things often tend to be quite different for widowers, whose social lives often carry on much as before, almost regardless of their age.

Indeed, some widowers find that if anything their social lives even expand, and a number of men have commented to me that they were exhausted by being asked out for lunch and supper nearly every day in the months after their spouse died. As the saying goes, a spare man is always welcome.

Nevertheless, whatever the state of your social life, the fact is that you are now alone, and this hits you hard, often at inopportune moments. Going out alone to social occasions, whether a meal with friends or a visit to the cinema, or even to a gathering of your own family, can occasionally be daunting, bringing home as it does the fact that it's now just you. Both widows and widowers have told me that it is often when they are in a room full of friends that they feel at their most lonely.

On the subject of loneliness, it might sometimes be helpful to bear in mind an old Irish saying: 'I'm not alone. I have myself.'

Miscellaneous thoughts and maxims

What follows is a miscellaneous assortment of thoughts that I have picked up along the way, from both widows and widowers.

Someone commented to a bereaved person that time heals. 'No it doesn't,' came the answer. 'But time helps you cope better.'

'The second year is the worst. That's when the reality sinks in.'

'Allow yourself to feel all the bewildering feelings. Don't suppress them, but don't indulge in them either.'

'Being a widow is not an illness.'

How do you reply to the question 'How are you?' Realising that most people do not really want to hear the details, one bereaved person has discovered a neat solution, and to this question invariably replies: 'It depends.' Always said with a smile.

Treasure your friends.

In the first few years, accept as many invitations as you can, and try to be a really good guest. If you continually turn down invitations from friends, they will eventually conclude that you are not interested, or that you wish to be left alone.

'You will know when you need a quiet day at home.'

'Be gentle with yourself. Spoil yourself. Don't rush.'

'Going to work saved me.'

A thought expressed by the journalist Felicity Green: 'I have plenty of people to do things with. I just have no one to do nothing with.'

'KBO,' as Winston Churchill said. In other words: keep buggering on.

Somerset Maugham advised: 'To acquire the habit of reading is to construct for yourself a refuge from almost all the miseries of life.'

'Keep neat, busy, and talking,' recommends one widower.

After his wife passed away, a widower recorded a number of messages that she had left on their answering machine at home, and kept this recording on his smartphone so that he could listen to it whenever he wished to hear the sound of her voice.

A widower writes: 'When I learnt that my wife had cancer of the lymph glands, the doctors said that we had just two years left together. In the event, it was ten years, and the greatest compliment that my wife paid me, and the greatest compliment that anyone is ever likely to pay me, was: "You prolonged my life."'

A widower's daughter said, 'We are all travelling on a long journey, but in separate cars.'

One widower thought, 'For me, to marry again would be abhorrent.'

In the aftermath of your wife's death, you will inevitably be absent-minded and do some foolish things.

A widower writes: 'I wish I had told her more often that I loved her. I never said it often enough.'

And: 'I thought that I would go before her, because I am older. I never imagined this loneliness.'

Don't try to be too brave.

If a friend invites you to go along to some event that is outside your comfort zone, say yes. It might just change your life.

Widowerhood is tricky.

Part IV

The years after she dies

Remembering

I once met a feisty military type who had been a widower for ten years or so. Before long I found myself asking him about his life as a widower, and I fear that at some stage I used the word 'forget'. He swelled up like a bullfrog and firmly informed me that being a widower was not about forgetting but about remembering. He was absolutely right, of course. One mustn't be afraid of remembering.

However, memories can at times be painful, because you know they will never be repeated. 'Why do we love, when losing hurts so much?' asks C.S. Lewis's wife Joy in *Shadowlands*, a film directed by Richard Attenborough. 'The greater the love, the greater the pain,' she continues.

One widower who contacted me said that he feels the same way. 'I almost feel that if one ever loses that pain, then some of the love will be lost,' he wrote. 'Far from upsetting me, that feeling of unhappiness is – curiously – reassuring. Our love was so secure that it has sustained me through the five years I have been widowed; and the pain is an essential part of it. It tells me that I am not alone, and it gives me strength and helps me to help others. To quote Plato: "Be kind, for everyone you meet is fighting a hard battle."'

> **Tip** If the memory of happy years of marriage is too painful, it can sometimes be a good idea to try out new patterns of living that do not continually remind you of times spent together with your spouse.

To further illustrate the risks involved in repeating patterns established with your deceased partner: a widow made the mistake of going to a concert very soon after her husband's death. They had regularly shared this pleasure together, but she then found herself sitting beside the only empty seat in the entire concert hall. She left in the interval.

Consolations

You can watch any programme on the television; listen to any radio programme; see any film at the cinema; go to any play or concert; any time you choose. You can eat anything, or nothing, any time you wish to. You can go to bed at any time, or stay in bed as long as you want. In short, you are an entirely free agent – even though you will often wonder whether this is a good thing. You now have the opportunity to create new ideas of how you wish to live. You can also choose to spend your money in whatever way you want, and without having to consider the needs of your spouse.

One widower lists the following consolations:

- I can watch *Match of the Day* every Saturday night without shouts from upstairs ordering me to bed.
- I am spared constant comments about my weight.
- When I go to a restaurant, no longer do I have to go through the menu dish by dish to check whether they have garlic in them.

He added that he would willingly have given up these consolations in perpetuity, just to have her back.

Tip Be a bit selfish and enjoy your new life.

Dating and remarriage

In my previous book, which was addressed to widows (rather than to widowers), possibly the most important tip was not to sell or to move house in the first year of widowhood. In the present book, the following tip is perhaps the most important of all. And that is: do not get remarried in a hurry, and most especially not in the first year. The reason I say this is that some widowers find the loneliness so devastating, and are so used to being looked after, that the thought of another person easing this pain and caring for them is very attractive. As a consequence, they rush into a second marriage, which they later regret. The inadvisability of getting remarried straight away is something for which there is endless anecdotal evidence, and against which doctors and grief counsellors strongly advise.

Grief takes its own time and you cannot rush it. Remarriage won't make your grief go away faster. Even if the idea of remarrying soon after the death of your wife and to a person you have known for many years is appealing, it is still inadvisable, as you will inevitably drag your suitcase of unprocessed grief into the next relationship.

Example 1 One widower wrote to me and said that now that he was on his own he felt the need to find out who he really was, and this involved learning to stand on his own two feet, questioning his beliefs, testing his capabilities, finding new friends and new interests, and also enjoying a few love affairs. Only after this, he felt, could he truly give himself to that special person and enter into a relationship without lies.

Example 2 My next example concerns two people, one a widow and the other a widower. During the time when their respective spouses had been terminally ill, both had supported each other, and later, when their spouses were dead, they realised that they were in love. However, they wisely decided to wait a while before they got married.

Example 3 A girlfriend of mine went out with a widower of five months. They got on like a house on fire. However, after he met her family and friends, he told her that he didn't think it was working. 'You're not like my wife,' he said. At this early stage of his widowerhood, he was looking for a replacement, not for a woman in her own right. What a tragedy for the two of them that they met so soon after the death of his wife.

Example 4 A gay widower wrote to say that he jumped into a new relationship a few months after the death of his long-term partner and before he had had time to grieve for him. The new relationship eventually came to end, and he now finds himself grieving not only for his most recent loss, but also for the earlier partner, whose death he had not grieved properly in the first place.

Before marriage, of course, comes dating. Some widowers will join dating agencies, others hope to meet another compatible soul socially. However, other men have said they would never marry again. Others too (and here I am referring to men of a certain age and generation) have told me that they find it impossible to be 'just friends' with attractive single women.

Other widowers find that they need a good length of time before they can consider any new relationship. 'My experience was that the living of grief was fundamental to my rediscovery of – and reconnection with – who I was and what my life meant,' one widower wrote. 'I became stronger and better able to sustain the weight of almost permanent despair, which itself began to lift; although for a long time I continued to have periods of deep gloom. I hate the phrase "move on", because it implies leaving behind and forgetting. Crucially, the wonderful thing is that you will always have her with you. Life becomes not an "instead of" but an "as well as". After two years I was wonderfully fortunate to find a glorious Other, one who forgives me for occasionally calling her by my first wife's name!'

Quiche and crampons: 'wolves surrounding the laager'

It is a truism that men are particularly susceptible to flattering attention from women, and this is especially the case for newly widowed men, who are all too often defenceless in the face of any show of kindness. Some widowers who are reasonably well off and good looking attract the occasional predatory single woman, who makes herself indispensable, turning up at all hours with quiche or some other goody, her crampons sharpened. Such 'helpfulness' can blind a lonely and vulnerable widower, especially in the early days, and women of this type have even been seen attending memorial services in search of a suitable widower. Many widowers have told me that they had found themselves in this situation, but that luckily they had recognised it in time, and had ended the relationship.

> **Tip** Do recognise that this happens, and keep your eyes open.

Example 1 An extreme case of this is the story of a newly widowed man who went on a two-week cruise and returned with a younger woman who was now wearing the engagement ring of his dead wife.

Example 2 One widower, the wealthy chairman of two banks in Europe, realised that after only two dates with any woman, he was put under considerable pressure to make matters permanent. He escaped, lived in a monastery for six months, and prayed with the monks between four and six o'clock each morning, after which his chauffeur collected him and drove him to work, returning him to the monastery for the evening. He used this special time to grieve for his beloved wife, who had died of cancer. He has since then happily remarried.

Example 3 Another widower referred to the women in his local church as 'wolves surrounding the laager' and tells me that one woman in particular – the most pious of them all – made it clear that she would have liked to 'go the Full Monty' with him, as he put it. He didn't take her up on her kind offer.

Remarriage and your children

If, after the death of your wife, you find another woman with whom you really wish to share your life, be aware that sometimes this can cause anxiety or much worse for either your or her children. (It is usually about money or property.) You always hope that your children would wish you to be happy and cared for, but this doesn't always happen.

For example, shortly after the death of his wife, a well-to-do widower married a much younger woman from a modest background. She now lives with him in his large house, where she rules the roost. Not only does she have no relationship with the man's children, but she also makes it difficult for him to see them.

> **Tip** If you do marry again, try not to let this come between you and your children.

Let me expand briefly on the topic of money and remarriage. Especially if the widower is wealthy, it is perfectly natural that his children should be concerned for their inheritance, and it is by no means materialistic of them to reflect that the arrival of a new woman on the scene might well mean that half of their father's estate will now go to the new wife, and thereafter to her children, and not to them. In other words, regardless of the woman's qualities as a person, and regardless of the happiness she might bring to the widower, from the financial point of view her arrival is inevitably a threat to the existing children. Not only this, but they might also see her as a threat from the emotional point of view. So, where the children are concerned, remarriage can be fraught with difficulty.

> **Tip** Your children might be largely reassured if you enter into a legal agreement confirming their inheritance in the event that you die before your new spouse.

It is not only your children whose approval it is good to have if you decide to get remarried. As often as not, your family – even your extended family – will wish to have a say. When one widower took his prospective wife to meet his family, the poor woman was given a thorough grilling; and the same thing happened to *him* when he met *her* family. 'Luckily we both passed muster,' he told me, 'and the wedding was allowed to go ahead.' As this same widower said: 'It is, of course, crucial to have the close family's approbation for a serious new relationship.'

Part V

When you die

A practical approach
to your own death

We now come to the matter of what happens when your own time comes.

I will start with something so apparently obvious that you might not think it worth saying. However, an astonishing number of people forget to make a will and consequently die intestate, to use the technical expression. For those whom the deceased leaves behind, this creates a whole range of very considerable difficulties that invariably have to be sorted out at great expense. How simple, on the other hand, to make a will. It costs next to nothing and takes very little time.

As I said earlier, it is not the purpose of this book to be too prescriptive or to set out too many dos and don'ts. However, I cannot emphasise enough that if you have not already made a will, you really *must* do so. Indeed, it is a widely shared view that, for the reasons outlined above, to fail to do so is in fact an act of selfishness towards those who come after you.

Similarly, it is a wise idea to arrange for a trusted figure to be given power of attorney over your affairs in the event that you become mentally incapacitated. If you fail to do this, your affairs will be run not by a person of your own choosing, but by the Court of Protection.

Bearing all this in mind, it is most advisable, as a widower, to write down the key information about your affairs, to update it annually and to make it known to your next of kin, so that when you die, it will be as easy as possible for your heirs and executors to sort out your estate.

What follows is a summary of the things to be considered.

- **Will**. Who has it? Who are the solicitors and executors? Is there a letter setting out your wishes? If there is, you should be aware that it is *not* a legally binding document, so you should be sure to choose executors on whom you can rely to carry out your wishes after you die.
- **Bank account 1**. While husband and wife are both alive, you should make sure that you have a joint account, since any account in the name of the deceased only will automatically be frozen at the time of death.
- **Bank account 2**. A top accountant writes: 'For the survivor, have one account in joint names (as signatories) with a trusted friend or family member, so that the account does not have to go through probate or administration. This account will pass to the remaining signatory by survivorship and will remain as an active account, available to the survivor. For Inheritance Tax purposes, the account will still form part of the estate, but will not be part of the will, and it will not be frozen. If the account is a non-interest-earning account, there should be no complication for you or the joint owner; and it could prove useful in the event of the survivor's incapacity, whether temporary or long term.'
- **Insurance**. For travel, health, critical illness, life, buildings. You should leave a detailed list of your insurance for all these things, including names, contact details, and reference numbers for the various brokers and companies involved.
- **Shares and other investments**. List details of all holdings and name(s) of your stockbroker(s) and financial advisers.

- **Pension**. Ditto.
- **Safety deposit box**. Location of key, and preferably give joint access to the box following your death.
- **Property**. Write down all details concerning landlords, mortgages, letting agents and the location of all title deeds.
- **Wife's jewellery**. You might wish to allocate this immediately after she dies. Speak to your accountant about any tax implications.
- **Clothing and personal effects**. Who should go through them and dispose of them? Do regular wardrobe clear-outs, remembering what you are leaving behind.
- **Papers and documents**. Sort and shred or file away regularly, so that everything is as clear and as trouble-free as possible for your heirs and executors.
- **Photos**. For the benefit of those who come after you, it is a nice idea to go through your old photos, writing down on the back who is who in them, or naming and filing any digital photos so they are easily recognisable.
- **Children**. If you are a young widower, designate a preferred guardian for your children.
- **Pets**. Ditto.
- **Gifts**. You can give away up to £3,000 a year tax-free (not £3,000 per recipient, but £3,000 in total). It is only sensible to use this allowance; whilst of course not going short yourself. (For more details, see the Appendix, page 73.)
- **Mementos**. Who would appreciate one?
- **Passwords and codes on your computer**. Leave a list of these, together with any other helpful advice about opening files.
- **Arguments and rifts**. Resolve if possible.
- **Funeral and burial or cremation**. Leave clear instructions for these, as well as the funds to pay for them.
- **Create a living will**. Doctors will do everything in their power to keep you alive, even when death is imminent. If

you do not wish them to prolong your life beyond its natural duration, you should consider writing a living will.

- **Power of attorney**. As mentioned above, do discuss power of attorney. In the event that you as a widower are no longer capable of managing your own affairs, power of attorney to allow others to do so should be in place. You should think about this as soon as you can after becoming a widower. Do keep on asking detailed questions and explanations of your accountant and solicitor.

Put information concerning all the above in one single, secure place, and tell your solicitor or trusted confidant where it is. Do not, in other words, divulge this information before you die.

Lastly, a few more words regarding the financial practicalities that must be faced by those left behind when *both* spouses or partners are gone. The following two examples apply equally to the surviving spouse, whether widow or widower.

- Example 1 The son of a wealthy couple had to spend over a year sorting out the intricacies of the tax situation left by his two elderly parents, and had to spend £60,000 of his own money to cover the cost (professional fees, etc.) of this process. (As I say, the son's parents were very comfortably off.) When, finally, probate was complete, he got his money back. But what if he hadn't been able to find it in the first place?
- Example 2 This applies equally to widowers and widows. An elderly widow knew that she was going to die imminently,

and therefore gave her daughter a cheque for £15,000 to cover the expenses that would inevitably be incurred in the aftermath of her death. 'Put it into your account now,' she said to her daughter, 'and make sure it is cleared before I die.' The bank cleared it eight hours before she died; if they hadn't cleared it in time, the cheque would have been worthless.

Appen

Appendix

Gifts

At the time of writing (2015), the annual exemption for gifts that will not be accumulated with the estate at death is £3,000. In plain English, this means that you can give away a total of £3,000 every year with no tax implications. If you do not use this exemption, it can be carried forward one year.

There are also permitted unlimited gifts. One can give away separate sums of £250 to any number of individuals in one year. In theory, therefore, the entire estate could be disposed of with no Inheritance Tax being due, provided that no one recipient receives more than £250 in any one year. Note, too, that the £250 cannot be added to the £3,000 tax-exempt gift to give one person a total of £3,250. The rule is £250 per recipient.

Furthermore, where an individual has excess income over their normal expenditure as required to maintain their usual standard of living, that individual is allowed to give away all or any part of that excess without its being regarded as a gift for the purposes of Inheritance Tax. However, such gifts have to be 'normal' for the donor. In other words, a miser (for example) would not be able to demonstrate that exceptional acts of generosity should be tax-exempt.

Lastly, the annual £3,000 and the gifts out of income can be made to individuals and/or organisations, whereas the £250 gifts must be to individuals.

Joint bank accounts

A competent accountant writes: 'I agree absolutely that the general expenditure account should be a joint account.

'What is also appropriate is for the widower to immediately bring in another member of the family into a joint account, so that it will remain operational if the widower were to become incapacitated.

'Unless you chose and declare otherwise, the value of that account will be regarded by HMRC as 50 per cent the widower's and 50 per cent the nominated family member's, but if the account is only receiving income and paying out living expenses, that should not be an issue.

'It is possible for the nominated family member to be no more than an authorised signatory; whereas a joint bank account in the names of husband and wife will only ever be regarded as owned fifty-fifty.'

Your accountant

As previously stated, it cannot be emphasised enough that it is inadvisable in the extreme to change your accountant shortly after your spouse dies. Furthermore, where the accountant has been the adviser and financial confidant of either spouse, there is a professional duty to assist the surviving spouse and family members with regard to their affairs.

As regards understanding the financial affairs of the deceased, you should not allow yourself to be intimidated by the complexities. Any professional or expert should be able to explain, in simple English, the effects of any situation of which they are supposed to have detailed knowledge.

Acknowledgements

My thanks to the various widowers who wrote to me about their experiences. I am deeply grateful to all the following:

- André
- Bob
- Chris
- Dave
- David x 3
- George
- Hermann
- Jeremy
- Dr John
- Nick
- Ralph
- Richard
- Roger
- Terry

My thanks, as always, to Sebastian Cresswell-Turner for his invaluable help in creating this book, and for his unflagging assistance in every aspect of it from beginning to end.

Further thanks to Caroline Stanley for her advice on the adminstrative practicalities of death; to Gill Kind and Melanie Hoffstead for advising about grief; and to Alan Ford for fact-checking, and advice on money matters.

Poems

On the death of Elizabeth Soane

Eternal Father! Thou, whence all proceeds
Of woe or joy that marks this mingled state
Of transient being, look in mercy down,
To soothe and heal his lacerated heart;
And through the weary lapse of ling'ring time
Support him, till that welcome hour arrive
Which grants re-union in a better world!

Anon., on the death in 1815 of Elizabeth Soane, wife of
the architect John Soane

Ode to Kath

I am alone, now I know it's true
There was a time when we were two
Those were the days when we would chat
Doing little jobs of this and that
We'd go to the shops and select our meals
But now I'm alone I know how it feels
To try and cook or have meals on wheels
The rooms are empty, there's not a sound
Sometimes I'm lost and wander around
To look for jobs that I can do
To bring back the days when we were two
When darkness falls and curtains drawn
That's when I feel most forlorn
But I must be honest and tell the truth
I'm not quite alone and here's the proof
Because beside me in her chair
She quietly waits our time to share
Kath said to me some time ago
Darling when the time comes for us to go
Let's mix our ashes and be together
So we can snuggle up for ever and ever.

Bob Lowe

Untitled

If I should die and leave you,
Be not like others, quick undone,
Who keep long vigil by the silent dust and weep.
For my sake turn to life and smile,
Nerving thy heart and trembling hand to comfort
weaker souls than thee.
Complete these unfinished tasks of mine
And I, perchance, may therein comfort thee.

Attributed to Thomas Gray

Splendour in the Grass

What though the radiance which was once so bright
Be now for ever taken from my sight,
Though nothing can bring back the hour
Of splendour in the grass, of glory in the flower,
We will grieve not, rather find
Strength in what remains behind.

William Wordsworth

Baucis and Philemon

One of the most famous stories recounted by the Roman poet Ovid in his *Metamorphoses* tells of two elderly country-dwellers, Baucis and Philemon, who were visited by Jupiter and his son Mercury, disguised as mortals and in search of shelter. Everywhere they had been turned away, but the good Baucis and Philemon took them in, and despite their poverty, gladly offered the gods everything they had. 'As often as the wine-bowl was drained, it was refilled of its own will,' says Ovid. 'Astonished by this strange occurrence, Baucis and the timid Philemon begged for forgiveness for the meal and their own unpreparedness,' he continues, and they offered to slaughter their one and only goose, which acted as guardian of their humble abode.

At this point, Jupiter and Mercury revealed themselves as gods, turned the hut into a temple, and asked the old couple what they wished for. Again in Ovid's words: 'We ask to be priests and to watch over your temple,' replied Philemon, the husband. 'Also, let the same hour take us both, and let me never see my wife's tomb, nor be buried by her.' This wish was granted, and one day not long afterwards, when they were standing together in front of the temple, each noticed that the other was turning into a tree. 'Farewell, spouse,' they said to each other as the bark slowly covered them. As Ovid recounts, even today the local inhabitants point out the two intertwining trees, one an oak and the other a linden.

For your notes

A note on the author

Jan Robinson began collecting advice from widows after her husband died. Six months later, she decided to turn this into a book and sell it through her website. *Tips From Widows* was picked up by Bloomsbury and published in 2015; *Tips from Widowers* is the companion volume. She has four children, seven grandchildren and lives in London.

tipsfromwidows.co.uk